The Lost Railways of County Durham

by Bernard Byrom

Ex-Great Western Railway 'Castle' Class No. 7029
Clun Castle passing Durham South signal box
with a railtour from the south of England in 1967.

Acknowledgements
The publisher wishes to thank the following for contributing photographs to this book: John Alsop for the front cover and pages 4, 6, 7, 10, 11, 13, 15, 16, 17, 18, 19, 20 (upper), 21 (both), 22, 23, 24, 25, 26, 28, 29, 30, 31, 32, 33, 34, 36, 38, 39, 40, 41, 43, 44, 45, 46 and the back cover. ; and Richard Casserley for pages 5, 8, 20 (lower), 27.

High Westwood Station.

Introduction

County Durham is regarded as the cradle of railways with good reason. Coal had been mined there for centuries and transported to the coast or to the Tyne and Wear rivers in chaldron wagons drawn by horses on crude waggonways laid on wooden rails. Matters improved in the early nineteenth century when cast-iron rails were introduced and stationary steam engines were developed to haul wagons up steep inclines along the routes but it was not until the promoters of the Stockton & Darlington Railway showed sufficient confidence in a new mode of propulsion - a mobile steam locomotive that had been developed principally by local man George Stephenson - that the railways we know today were born.

The area was rich in minerals that were essential to the Industrial Revolution. These were principally coal for heating and stoking factory boilers, and iron ore and limestone for ironmaking and shipbuilding. Once quiet fishing villages became ports that soon began to export coal on an unimaginable scale today and this lasted far into the twentieth century.

Even before the advent of passenger railways the county was criss-crossed by a network of privately owned waggonways, all heading for staithes (short piers with rails for coal wagons to reach the colliers) on the Tyne or Wear rivers or coastal villages. The conveyance of passengers was almost an afterthought; mineral traffic was what really mattered and passengers were often considered an inconvenience. Indeed, the passenger service on many lines developed out of an initial service for miners and their families.

The history of the passenger railways in County Durham is very complex. Whilst the main passenger routes ran from north to south, the freight lines generally ran from west to east and this resulted in a criss-crossing of several lines, many of which spawned competing branches. The lines featured in this book were built by a variety of independent companies who were all ultimately incorporated into the mighty North Eastern Railway which, by the end of the nineteenth century, had a complete monopoly of all the railways in the county. In the 1840s George Hudson, the 'Railway King', was the driving force behind the amalgamation of smaller railways in his ambition to forge a railway link between the Thames and the Tweed. The unorthodox (and illegal) practices he used to achieve this led to his downfall in 1849 but out of this arose the formation of the North Eastern Railway in 1854 by the amalgamation of four large railway companies; these were the York & North Midland Railway, the York, Newcastle & Berwick Railway, the Leeds Northern Railway, and the Malton & Driffield Railway. In the following decades the North Eastern swallowed up the remaining independent lines in County Durham including the Stockton & Darlington, the Durham & Sunderland, the Hartlepool Dock & Railway Company and, finally, the Londonderry, Seaham & Sunderland Railway.

In the nineteenth century ironworks were developed on both sides of the Pennines but each side depended on natural resources from the other side. Durham coal was of a very high quality and very suitable for conversion into coke which was the fundamental fuel for the smelting of iron in the blast furnaces situated in the Furness area of Lancashire where rich iron ore deposits were geographically remote from supplies of coal and coke. Conversely the poorer quality iron ore deposits of the Cleveland Hills needed to be supplemented by the richer iron ore of the Furness and West Cumberland areas for the blast furnaces on Teesside. A line across the Pennines connecting the two areas was obviously necessary; this was built over Stainmore and at its peak in the late nineteenth century this traffic reached over a million tons a year.

Most travellers nowadays, as they speed over the East Coast Main Line between Darlington and Newcastle via Durham, do not realise that until 1872 the main line to Newcastle completely bypassed Durham and took an earlier route that is still in existence but has been 'mothballed' by Railtrack since 1991.

This book covers the lines in County Durham that once carried a passenger service. Because of the very nature of these services the line sections are sometimes fragmented because that is exactly how these services operated, criss-crossing the county with their branches being cut back according to traffic flows, economic considerations and, finally, the 'Beeching Axe'.

Darlington — Barnard Castle

Passenger service withdrawn	30 November 1964
Distance	16 ½ miles
Company	Darlington & Barnard Castle Railway

Stations closed	Date of closure
Piercebridge	30 November 1964
Winston	30 November 1964
Gainford	30 November 1964
Broomielaw	30 November 1964
Barnard Castle	30 November 1964 (see Bishop Auckland to Barnard Castle)

Broomielaw Station, c.1905.

As early as 1832 there were a number of proposals to build a branch line from Barnard Castle to join the Stockton & Darlington Railway somewhere between Shildon and Darlington, but these proposals were blocked in turn by both the first and second Dukes of Cleveland who owned most of the land around Barnard Castle. They particularly opposed the suggestion that the line should run from Barnard Castle to West Auckland because this would have cut their estate in two. Even when the route was changed to run from Barnard Castle to Darlington the second Duke still opposed the Bill and it was lost in Parliament in 1853; however, it was approved in the following year and the Darlington & Barnard Castle Railway Act was granted on 3 July 1854. The first sod was cut on 20 July that year and the line, which had no engineering or physical features of note, opened on 8 July 1856.

The line commenced at a junction with the Stockton & Darlington main line at Hopetown, just northwest of Darlington North Road station and ended at a terminal station in Barnard Castle. However, after the South Durham & Lancashire Union Railway opened its line from a second terminus at Barnard Castle to Tebay on 8 August 1861 it was decided to make the Barnard Castle station into a joint through station and this was opened on 1 May 1862. The Darlington & Barnard Castle Railway's old station became a goods station which remained open until the end of freight services on the line in 1965, and which survives to this day although much altered and extended. The new station consisted of a single through platform with a bay at either end, with the central part of the platform covered by an overall roof. Nearby was a two-road engine shed that opened in 1865 and closed in 1937.

Goods traffic was the mainstay of the line and was very much two-way, iron ore from the Barrow-in-Furness area being carried eastbound to the blast furnaces of Teesside and coke and coal being carried in the opposite direction to the Furness district. By 1910, with both companies having been part of the North Eastern Railway since the early 1860s, there were seven passenger trains each way on weekdays between Darlington and Barnard Castle, three of these running through to Tebay and Penrith; forty years later the service was virtually the same. Apart from the regular passenger service it was also a popular summer excursion route between the northeast and Blackpool to where Saturdays-only through trains were first introduced in 1932. Another regular train was an army special that ran from Broomilaw to Preston every Friday and returned on Monday.

Engine No. 899 with the 1.03 p.m. service from Penrith to Darlington at Barnard Castle Station, 4 June 1935.

Class J21 0-6-0 engines were generally used on the line, sometimes double-heading trains because of weight restrictions on the viaducts west of Barnard Castle although these restrictions were considerably eased in 1954 and allowed the use of BR Standard Class 4MT 2-6-0 locomotives. DMUs (diesel multiple units) were introduced on passenger services on 3 February 1958 and the number of weekday services was increased to eleven in each direction, four of these being Kirkby Stephen or Penrith trains, four Middleton-in-Teesdale trains and three starting or terminating at Barnard Castle. However, by 1961 the service had been reduced to seven weekday trains plus one on Mondays only from Darlington to Barnard Castle, with eight weekday trains plus two Saturdays only in the opposite direction.

The line closed to passengers on 30 November 1964 and the track was lifted in the following year. The station house at Piercebridge is now a private house, as is the goods shed and its associated buildings. The station houses at Gainford and Winston plus the crossing keeper's dwelling at the latter station are also private houses but all the station buildings on the line have been totally demolished apart from Broomielaw.

Bishop Auckland — Barnard Castle

Passenger service withdrawn	18 June 1962
Distance	15 miles
Company	South Durham & Lancashire Union Railway

Stations closed	*Date of closure*
West Auckland *	18 June 1962
Evenwood	14 October 1957
Cockfield Fell **	15 September 1958
Barnard Castle	30 November 1964

* Named St Helens from opening on 1 December 1833 to 1 March 1878.
** Originally called Cockfield until 1 July 1923.

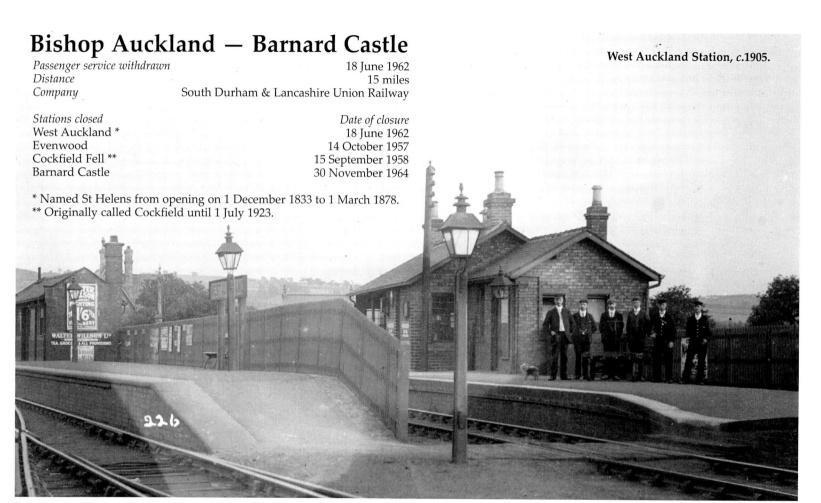

On 17 July 1857 the South Durham & Lancashire Union Railway Act was passed after encountering very little Parliamentary opposition. This Act authorised the construction of a line between the Stockton & Darlington Railway, at Spring Gardens Junction near St Helens on its Bishop Auckland to Haggerleases Colliery branch, and the Lancaster & Carlisle Railway at Tebay, with a connection at Barnard Castle to the Darlington & Barnard Castle Railway. Initially only the Barnard Castle to Tebay section was built and all traffic to Bishop Auckland had to be worked round via Shildon until the line between Barnard Castle and Spring Gardens Junction was opened for passenger traffic on 1 August 1863. By the time the line opened the South Durham & Lancashire Union Railway had been taken over by the Stockton & Darlington Railway which was itself swallowed up by the North Eastern Railway on 13 July 1863, less than three weeks before this section of line opened.

The main purpose of the line was to take coke to the Cumberland and Furness blast furnaces and iron ore back to Cleveland. The source of the coke was around Bishop Auckland and between 1861 and 1863 coke trains had to be routed via Darlington to reach Barnard Castle and the South Durham line because the section between Bishop Auckland and Barnard Castle was not yet completed.

In 1902 there were six weekday passenger trains in each direction using the line, plus a seasonal one from Barnard Castle to Bishop Auckland at 7.44 p.m. In 1910 there were five trains but by 1953 these had been reduced to two; by the time the line closed in 1962 the service had been still further reduced to two trains from Bishop Auckland to Barnard Castle and only one in the opposite direction. The line was also traversed by seasonal and excursion through trains between the Northeast and the Lancashire resorts of Blackpool and Morecambe. One interesting working was an unpublicised passenger train that ran from Durham to Ulverston on alternate Fridays taking injured and sick miners to the National Union of Mineworkers convalescent home at Conishead Priory. Its normal route from Durham was via Bishop Auckland, Barnard Castle, Kirkby Stephen and Tebay. Through passenger services were withdrawn from the line on 12 June 1962.

The shed at Barnard Castle Station, 4 June 1935.

In London & North Eastern Railway days (1923 to 1947) passenger services were mainly worked by Classes J21 and J25 0-6-0s, replaced in the 1950s by BR Standard Class 2-6-0s and 2-6-2Ts. In January 1958 DMUs took over local services although steam was retained on summer through trains.

Wear Valley Junction — Wearhead

Passenger service withdrawn	29 June 1953
Distance	22 miles
Company	Wear Valley Junction to Frosterley: Wear Valley Railway
	Frosterley to Stanhope: Frosterley & Stanhope Railway
	Stanhope to Wearhead: Stockton & Darlington Railway

Stations closed	*Date of closure*
Wear Valley Junction *	8 July 1935
Witton-le-Wear **	29 June 1953
Harperley	29 June 1953
Wolsingham	29 June 1953

Stations closed	*Date of closure*
Frosterley	29 June 1953
Stanhope	29 June 1953
Eastgate	29 June 1953
Westgate-in-Weardale	29 June 1953
St John's Chapel	29 June 1953
Wearhead	29 June 1953

* Originally named Witton Junction until May 1872.
** Originally named Witton until March 1852.

An 0-6-0 engine with a train from Wearhead entering Wolsingham Station, c.1951.

The Wear Valley was rich in limestone deposits, particularly in the area around Frosterley and Bishopley. The Wear Valley Railway Act was passed on 31 July 1845 to construct a line from Wear Valley Junction (at that time called Witton Junction) on the Bishop Auckland & Weardale Railway to Frosterley, with a connecting branch to Bishopley. The line opened on 3 August 1847 and the Wear Valley Railway Company had ambitions to extend the line further up Weardale to Alston and from there on to Carlisle but this plan had to be abandoned because of the company's depressed financial situation. However, the line was extended to Stanhope by the Frosterley & Stanhope Railway Act which was passed on 28 June 1861; the extension opened on 22 October 1862 and the whole line was then worked by the Stockton & Darlington Railway. The final extension of the line, many years later, was to Wearhead and was opened for traffic on 21 October 1895. The final six and a half miles progressively steepened, with very short intermissions, to 1 in 102/86/78 and finally 1 in 68.

Frosterley Station, *c*.1912.

In its heyday the line served huge quarries on both sides of the valley, particularly in the Broadwood and Bishopley areas, and there were many quarries on the hillsides beyond Frosterley. Limestone was quarried in vast quantities and was carried by the railway down to the ironworks in the Middlesborough area. However, quarrying in the Bishopley area declined rapidly after the First World War and the Bishopley branch, which had never had a passenger service, closed in 1928.

Stanhope Station.

The railway was basically a single-track line with passing loops and sidings at most stations. In 1900 there were six down and five up passenger trains daily running along the valley, with one in each direction between Wear Valley Junction and Stanhope on Sundays. Until 1935 the service on the branch was provided by coaches detached from Darlington to Blackhill trains and worked from Wear Valley Junction by one of the Class J21 0-6-0 branch engines stabled at Stanhope and Wearhead. However, in 1935 the pattern of services was changed and the Darlington to Blackhill trains were extended to Newcastle via the Derwent Valley line. The Wear Valley trains were now worked as a branch service from Bishop Auckland which allowed the closure of Wear Valley Junction shed, after which Wearhead shed worked the branch with a Class J21 0-6-0 engine until the passenger service was withdrawn. Stanhope shed, although closed in 1930, found a new lease of life during the Second World War when the historic locomotives 'Derwent' and 'Locomotion' were stored there for safety from Darlington Bank Top Station.

Freight services survived until 1961 when the line was cut back to St John's Chapel and again in 1968 to Eastgate which is the present terminus. Between 1988 and 1992 a summer Saturday only passenger train to Stanhope operated as an extension of the service from Darlington but in 1993 the line was mothballed. Fortunately the line was purchased in 2004 by Weardale Railways Limited who now run a service between Wolsingham and Stanhope. Railtrack have reinstated the connection at Bishop Auckland and Weardale Railways Limited intend to operate over the whole length of line between Bishop Auckland and Eastgate. The platforms at Wolsingham, Frosterley and Stanhope have been rebuilt and restored and the station buildings at the latter have been refurbished.

Bishop Auckland — Tow Law and Blackhill

Passenger service withdrawn	Tow Law to Blackhill: 1 May 1939	*Stations closed*	*Date of closure*
	Crook to Tow Law: 11 June 1956	Burnhill ***	1 May 1939
	Bishop Auckland to Crook: 8 March 1965	Rowley ****	1 May 1939
		Blackhill †	23 May 1955

Distance 21 ½ miles
Company Bishop Auckland to Crook: Bishop Auckland & Weardale Railway
Crook to Blackhill: Stockton & Darlington Railway

Stations closed	*Date of closure*
Etherley & Witton Park *	8 March 1965
Beechburn **	8 March 1965
Crook	8 March 1965
Tow Law	11 June 1956

* Originally named Etherley and Witton Park until 1 July 1871. Reopened and renamed Witton Park for Escomb on 25 August 1991 then closed in 1992.
** Originally named Howden until 16 April 1869.
*** Originally named Burn Hill Junction until 1 May 1893.
**** Originally named Cold Rowley until 1 July 1868.
† Opened as Blackhill then renamed Benfieldside on 2 December 1867, Consett on 1 November 1882, Consett and Blackhill on 1 May 1885, and reverting back to Blackhill on 1 May 1896.

Tow Law Station, *c.*1951.

The Bishop Auckland & Weardale Railway Act was passed on 15 July 1837 with the intention of tapping the mineral wealth of the Weardale area but it wasn't until 8 November 1843 that the line was opened as far as Crook and then only for goods traffic; passenger traffic didn't begin until 3 January 1844. The first station at Bishop Auckland built at this time was enlarged in December 1867 when a new north to east curve and platform were installed, followed around 1885 by a new north to west curve and platform. In 1905 a single platform was built on the 1867 north to west curve, converting the station into its familiar triangular formation. It was also notable for its large signal gantries which guarded the three approaches to the station, and also for the extra high North signal box.

The line was leased and worked by the Stockton & Darlington Railway and in 1845 it was extended from Crook via Tow Law to Waskerley to provide another outlet for the products of the Derwent Iron Company at Consett, necessitating building a new station at Crook about a quarter of a mile north of the original station. This new section of line was originally called the Weardale Extension Railway but later, under a merger with the line from Stanhope to Consett, it was known as the Wear & Derwent Junction Railway. The Bishop Auckland & Weardale Railway amalgamated with the Wear Valley Railway in 1847, then they in turn were taken over by the Stockton & Darlington Railway in 1858 and by the North Eastern Railway in 1863.

Rowley Station.

The extension northwards from Crook to Tow Law was built over very hilly country and was initially rope-worked over the Sunniside Incline with gradients almost two miles long at 1 in 13 and 1 in 16. Subsequently in 1867/68 a deviation line was built by the North Eastern Railway to ease the gradient and allow locomotives to work this section of the line which was built in the shape of a gigantic letter S and included four miles at 1 in 51 and 1 in 52 to climb the bank. A new station was opened on this line at Tow Law on 2 March 1868 and a junction station with the old line was opened at Burnhill.

In the North Eastern Railway's time a through service was begun from Darlington to Tyneside via Bishop Auckland, Crook, Tow Law, Burnhill and along the Derwent Valley line through Blackhill to join the

Blackhill Station.

Newcastle & Carlisle line near Blaydon. Trains were usually hauled by Classes A5 or A8 4-6-2T or L1 2-6-4T engines from Darlington, but with increasing competition from roads and the decline in the handling of lime and stone the line north of Tow Law to Blackhill was closed to passengers on 1 May 1939, along with the stations at Burnhill and Rowley. The line was further cut back to Crook on 11 June 1956 and the final section of line from Bishop Auckland to Crook closed to passengers on 6 March 1965, the track north of Wear Valley Junction being lifted around two years later. Even as late as 1961 there were still nineteen weekday trains in both directions between Bishop Auckland and Crook, all of them running to or from Darlington and occasionally Saltburn.

The station at Rowley had three platform faces, which were a side platform containing the station buildings and an island platform. In 1972 the station was dismantled and transported to Beamish where it was painstakingly rebuilt, stone by stone, and furnished as it would have been in 1913.

Etherley Station has an interesting history. It first appears in a timetable of September 1847 but the station was re-sited and reopened with a single platform on 16 October 1867. At that time it was called Etherley & Witton Park but after 1 July 1871 it became plain Etherley. It was closed to passengers on 8 March 1965 when the service between Bishop Auckland and Crook was withdrawn but was reopened on 25 August 1991 under the name of Witton Park and had a summer Saturday service to Stanhope. This service only lasted until the following year before being discontinued but the station is nowadays still intact and has been converted into a private residence.

What must have been one of the line's busiest events ever was the FA Amateur Cup Final in April 1954 when the finalists were Bishop Auckland and Crook Town, situated five miles apart and two of the most illustrious names in amateur football. They dominated the competition in the 1950s when, between them, they won the cup every single year between 1954 and 1959 with the exception of 1958. For the 1954 cup final played at Wembley Stadium thirteen eleven-coach trains ran from Bishop Auckland and Crook to London. The match was drawn and the replay was arranged for Easter Monday at Newcastle United's ground when eighteen specials were laid on. This match also ended in a draw and a second replay was arranged three days later at Middlesbrough's ground; this was on a working day so only nine specials were needed. What a contrast to today!

Newcastle — Blackhill, returning via Consett

Passenger service withdrawn	Newcastle to Blackhill: 1 February 1954
	Blackhill to East Coast Main Line at Birtley: 23 May 1955
Distance	37 miles
Company	Newcastle to Blackhill: Derwent Valley Railway
	Blackhill to East Coast Main Line: North Eastern Railway

Stations closed	*Date of closure*
Swalwell	2 November 1953
Rowlands Gill	1 February 1954
Lintz Green	2 November 1953
High Westwood	4 May 1942
Ebchester	21 September 1953
Shotley Bridge *	21 September 1953
Blackhill **	23 May 1955
Consett	23 May 1955

Stations closed	*Date of closure*
Leadgate	23 May 1955
Annfield Plain	23 May 1955
West Stanley ***	23 May 1955
Beamish	21 September 1953
Pelton	7 December 1953

Closed stations on the East Coast Main Line

Birtley	5 December 1955
Lamesley	4 June 1945
Low Fell	7 April 1952
Bensham	5 April 1954

* Originally named Snows Green until 1868.
** For naming history see Bishop Auckland to Tow Law and Blackhill section.
*** Originally named Sheild Row until 1 February 1934.

Rowlands Gill Station.

Work on the Derwent Valley Railway started in 1865 and the line was opened on 2 December 1867. It ran in a generally southwest direction from a junction with the Newcastle & Carlisle line at Derwenthaugh west of Scotswood and necessitated fairly heavy earthworks including a deep 880 yards long cutting near Rowlands Gill. Four viaducts were constructed including the 500 feet long Nine Arches Viaduct which was one of the major engineering feats of the railway; it had to be built because the Earl of Strathmore would not allow the railway to pass through his Gibside estate. The line was double track between the junction at Derwenthaugh and Lintz Green and single track between there and Blackhill. At the southern end of the line the North Eastern Railway constructed a new route in 1894 from South Pelaw to Annfield Plain that bypassed the rope-worked inclines built by the Stanhope & Tyne Railway on its line from Stanhope Quarries to South Shields.

A station building under construction beneath the line at High Westwood.

WESTWOOD. N.E.R.

Shotley Bridge Station.

The new route, which was extended to Consett in 1896, was worked by locomotive-hauled trains and led eventually to the introduction of a Newcastle to Blackhill service via Birtley and Consett which connected at Blackhill with the Newcastle to Durham service via Scotswood and Rowlands Gill. Blackhill was the busiest station on the line; a covered bay platform at the south end was provided for the Darlington trains and through platforms were used by trains from Newcastle via Scotswood which returned to Newcastle either via Consett and Annfield Plain or via Lanchester and Durham.

Consett Station, 28 September 1963.

Annfield Plain Station, *c.*1911.

Sheild Row Station (later West Stanley), June 1911.

The line traversed hilly country and the ruling gradient was 1 in 60 towards Blackhill, followed by downhill stretches at 1 in 66 on to Consett and several uphill miles at 1 in 50 towards Beamish and Pelton. It must have been quite a relief for train crews when the relative level of the East Coast Main Line was reached just south of Birtley.

At its peak in 1914 the railway was carrying over half a million passengers a year and had a regular goods traffic of timber, bricks and coal to Newcastle and iron ore to Consett. However, by the 1920s buses had started to take the passengers away from the railway. Even so, in 1925 the service still consisted of six trains in each direction on weekdays and twelve on Saturdays although some of these only ran between Consett and Newcastle. In 1928 Clayton steam railcars were introduced onto the line but were not successful and the line reverted to steam operation although Sentinel cars were also tried a few years later. Locomotives used on the branch in LNER days were mainly of Classes G5 0-4-4T and A8 4-6-2T but after nationalisation Classes J39 0-6-0 and K1 2-6-0 also appeared.

As post-war road haulage traffic became more efficient the line's passenger and freight service declined; by the summer of 1953 there were only three through trains outward via Rowlands Gill plus two (one on Saturdays only) that began their journey at Blackhill. In the opposite direction there were three trains that only ran as far as Blackhill plus an early morning service from Leadgate to Newcastle. The passenger services on the line were withdrawn in two stages in 1954 and 1955 and the line finally closed completely on 11 November 1963. The track was lifted in 1964 and for many years little was done to the line until Durham County Council developed it as a country park. The viaducts and bridges were repaired and the trackbed has now become an excellent country park and cycle route.

Blackhill — Durham (Lanchester Branch)

Passenger service withdrawn	1 May 1939
Distance	14 miles
Company	North Eastern Railway

Stations closed	Date of closure
Knitsley *	1 May 1939
Lanchester	1 May 1939
Witton Gilbert	1 May 1939
Bearpark **	1 May 1939

* Closed between 1 February 1916 to 30 March 1925.
** Originally named Aldin Grange until 19 June 1884; renamed as Aldin Grange for Bearpark until 11 May 1927.

Lanchester Station.

Ironworks were first established at Consett in 1841 and their requirements of limestone were initially conveyed from Middlesbrough and the neighbouring Cleveland Hills by circuitous rail links. By the 1860s Consett needed more direct access to its raw materials and to the port of Middlesbrough for its output and a route up the Browney Valley seemed the ideal location for such a line. Construction of the single-track Lanchester branch which ran from Relly Mill Junction, south of Durham, to join the Stockton & Darlington Railway south west of Consett, commenced in February 1861 and it officially opened the following year. In 1870 Lord Lambton who owned land in the Lanchester Valley accepted an application to search for coal which was found the following year so the North Eastern Railway doubled its track in anticipation of colliery demand. As well as a number of substantial stone bridges spanning the River Browney there was a 700-foot-long viaduct one and half miles east of Knitsley Station, built mainly of wood and towering 70 feet above the Knitsley Burn. By 1915 the viaduct was in need of major repairs and a decision was made to turn it into an embankment using colliery slag and old ballast. Gradients on the line fell quite steeply from Blackhill towards Lanchester with several sections at 1 in 60.

Passenger numbers were always light and this branch was an early casualty with the last passenger train running on 1 May 1939. However, its stations were occasionally used by Miners' Gala excursion trains after that date, the last recorded one being on 17 July 1954. The branch closed entirely in 1966 when minerals were diverted to road transport and Consett steel traffic was rerouted via Annfield Plain and Pelaw; the track was lifted in 1967. Since then the twelve-mile long western part of the branch has been converted into the Lanchester Valley railway path and cycleway running from Lydgetts Junction just south of Consett to the Broompark Picnic Area near Stonebridge.

Bishop Auckland — Ferryhill

Passenger service withdrawn Bishop Auckland to Spennymoor: 4 December 1939
Spennymoor to Ferryhill: 31 March 1952

Distance   9 ½ miles
Company   North Eastern Railway

Stations closed   *Date of closure*
Coundon   4 December 1939
Byers Green   4 December 1939

Stations closed   *Date of closure*
Spennymoor   31 March 1952
Ferryhill (East Coast Main Line)   6 March 1967
(see Ferryhill to Gateshead, Ferryhill to Port Clarence and Ferryhill to Hartlepool sections)

* Originally named Ferry Hill until *c.*1852

Byers Green Station, *c.*1920.

Ferryhill Station.

The West Durham Railway was the result of a line first placed before Parliament in 1835 under the title of the South Durham Railway. Its object was to provide an outlet to the east for the minerals of Weardale by joining up with the already sanctioned Byers Green branch of the Clarence Railway. The Bill was successful after three attempts and three name changes and an Act was granted on 4 July 1839 for a line five and a half miles long, mainly on inclines. However, the West Durham's area was also served by the Stockton & Darlington Railway so it was only natural that when both companies came into North Eastern Railway ownership the uneconomic duplication was eliminated and the West Durham's line was closed. This left the Byers Green branch as a dead-end at Tod Hills, three miles north of Bishop Auckland so in 1885 the North Eastern Railway built a link between Byers Green and Bishop Auckland at Burnhouse Junction. The line between here and Bishop Auckland was single track but that eastwards was double.

An intermittent passenger service had operated from Ferryhill to Tod Hills where the North Eastern Railway erected a new passenger station in 1878 and this service continued until 1885 when it was replaced by a Ferryhill to Bishop Auckland service via Coundon; this led to the area being served by a new Byers Green station on the new section of line. The North Eastern Railway also erected a three-road engine shed at Tod Hills but this was closed in 1922. In 1902 there were seven weekday trains in each direction plus an extra one on Wednesdays and Saturdays but traffic declined over the years and on 4 December 1939 the section between Spennymoor and Bishop Auckland was closed to passenger traffic, followed by the Ferryhill to Spennymoor section on 31 March 1952; by that time the service was being operated by a G5 0-4-4T working two push-and-pull coaches.

Durham — Waterhouses

Passenger service withdrawn	29 October 1951
Distance	5 ½ miles
Company	North Eastern Railway

Stations closed	*Date of closure*
Ushaw Moor	29 October 1951
Waterhouses	29 October 1951

Ushaw Moor Station.

The Dearness Valley Railway was incorporated by an Act of Parliament of 30 July 1855 and was sold to the North Eastern Railway on 13 July 1857. Although the line opened for goods on 1 January 1858 from Dearness Valley Junction on the Durham to Bishop Auckland line to a point near the junction of the Stanley incline and the line to East Hedleyhope Colliery, a passenger service wasn't introduced until 1 November 1877 when a single platform terminus was built part way along the line at the village of Esh Winning although the station was named Waterhouses and passenger trains never went beyond here. A second station on the line was added at Ushaw Moor on 1 September 1884.

LNER engine No. 1772 running round the 4.16 p.m. service from Durham at Waterhouses Station, 13 May 1936.

Several collieries were accessed from the branch and the passenger service on the line was always of secondary importance. In 1925 there were eight trains each way per day, the passengers being almost solely miners and their families travelling to Durham for shopping or pleasure. In the 1930s excursion trains used to run on Saturday nights to Newcastle with summer Saturday trips to Whitley Bay and South Shields. However, by October 1949 the passenger service had been reduced to one weekday train per day to Durham and the service was withdrawn altogether on 29 October 1951; the two passenger stations remained in use until the 1960s for occasional miners' gala trains with morning passenger trains taking bands, banners and passengers into Durham and bringing them back again in the afternoon. The freight service continued until the end of 1964.

The branch was double track from Dearness Valley Junction to New Brancepeth Colliery Junction, a quarter of a mile beyond Ushaw Moor station. The mineral service continued for three-quarters of a mile beyond Waterhouses Goods to Stanley Bank Foot and beyond that was a private line to East Hedleyhope colliery. Immediately west of Ushaw Moor Station was a wooden trestle viaduct and in 1902 a second wooden viaduct was built alongside, the first viaduct being demolished some years later and the second structure in the winter of 1967/68 when the track was lifted. The line has now been converted into the eight-mile Deerness Valley Railway Path which starts at the Broomhill Picnic Area and passes through the villages of Ushaw Moor and Esh Winning.

Bishop Auckland — Sunderland via Durham

Passenger service withdrawn	4 May 1964	*Stations closed*	*Date of closure*
Distance	26 miles	Leamside	5 October 1953 (see Ferryhill to Gateshead)
Company	North Eastern Railway	Fencehouses	4 May 1964 (see Ferryhill to Gateshead)
		Penshaw	4 May 1964 (see Ferryhill to Gateshead)
Stations closed	*Date of closure*	Cox Green	4 May 1964
Hunwick	4 May 1964	Hylton	4 May 1964
Willington	4 May 1964	Pallion	4 May 1964
Brancepeth	4 May 1964	Millfield	2 May 1955
Brandon Colliery	4 May 1964	Sunderland Fawcett Street	4 August 1879

Hunwick Station.

A line between Bishop Auckland and the northeast was first proposed in the Newcastle & Darlington Junction Act of 27 July 1846 but before work could start the company became part of the York & Newcastle Railway and, soon afterwards, the York, Newcastle & Berwick Railway. This company's Act for the Team Valley line, passed on 30 June 1848, included details of a new route for the Bishop Auckland branch that would leave the Team Valley line at Newton Hall and pass through Durham to Relly Mill, then run along the northern side of the Wear Valley. The present Durham station and viaduct are part of this line. As an aftermath of the financial scandal in 1849 that brought down George Hudson, 'The Railway King', work on the line was delayed and it was not until 1 April 1857 that it was ready for use throughout between Bishop Auckland and Leamside, which station it approached over the nine-arch Brasside viaduct and then joined the then main line between York and Newcastle.

The first railway to Bishop Auckland had opened in 1843 and the town eventually developed into an important interchange station with lines radiating to all parts of the railway network including Darlington, Blackhill (and on to Tyneside via the Derwent Valley), Weardale, Spennymoor, Barnard Castle, Middleton-in-Teesdale and Durham. These were accommodated by a systematic enlargement of the station; in December 1857 a new joint North Eastern Railway and Stockton & Darlington Railway station was opened adjacent to the original 1843 platform and in December 1867 this station was enlarged and a new north to east curve and platform were installed, and also a new north to west curve. The next move was to construct a second platform on the north to east curve, probably in 1885 in conjunction with the new line to Burnhouse Junction which allowed through running to Spennymoor and Ferryhill. There was also a connecting spur from the Crook line which bypassed the station and joined the Durham line north of the station. Finally in 1905 a single platform was built on the 1867 north to west curve, thus converting the station into a triangular formation. There were four roads through the station and the platforms had quite stylish verandas in front of the station buildings.

Bishop Auckland was also notable for its large signal gantries which guarded the three approaches to the station, and also for the extra high North signal box. The station was always busy – in 1925 the daily passenger service consisted of the following: nine trains to Crook, Tow Law and Blackhill, with six of these giving Wearhead branch connections at Wear Valley Junction; nine trains to Darlington; seven trains to Barnard Castle; ten trains to Durham and Sunderland; nine trains to Ferryhill; a similar number of trains in the opposite direction on each line. Class G5 0-4-4T locomotives were used on most trains.

Brancepeth Station.

The Durham line platforms curved sharply to the right on the north to west curve and the double-track line almost immediately passed through the 93-yard-long Bondgate Tunnel and then crossed the Wear Valley on the Newton Cap Viaduct of eleven 60-foot arches. The line opened to passenger traffic on 1 April 1857 and joined what is now the East Coast Main Line at Relly Mill Junction south of Durham where a line also trailed in from the left from the Lanchester Valley and Consett. The line also served a number of collieries and brickworks and was occasionally used as a diversionary route by main-line express traffic to avoid engineering works between Darlington and Durham.

The Act of 1846 had also authorised the Newcastle & Darlington Junction Railway to build a line from Penshaw to join the Durham & Sunderland Railway at Sunderland. This opened for passengers on 1 June 1853 and after the opening of the Bishop Auckland to Leamside branch it provided a through route between Durham and Sunderland. The Sunderland station was at Fawcett Street which was closed in 1879 when the present through station was opened.

At one time there were a number of through trains on the line but by 1961 there was only one daily through train in each direction, running between Bishop Auckland and Sunderland, plus another that ran eastwards on Mondays to Fridays. However, there were a number of trains to and from stations such as Newcastle, Darlington and even Leeds that used the two halves of the line as far as Durham before branching off onto one of the many lines radiating from there. Passenger services were withdrawn on 4 May 1964 and much of the western end of the line has been converted into the nine and a half mile Brandon – Bishop Auckland Railway Path that runs from the Broompark Picnic Area and ends at the Newton Cap Viaduct near Bishop Auckland.

Ferryhill — Gateshead via Leamside ('The Old Main Line')

Passenger service withdrawn	4 May 1964	*Stations closed*	*Date of closure*
Distance	23 ¼ miles	Belmont	1 April 1857
Company	4 separate companies: see below	Durham Gilesgate	1 April 1857
		Leamside	5 October 1953
		Fencehouses	4 May 1964
Stations closed	*Date of closure*	Penshaw	4 May 1964
Ferryhill (East Coast Main Line)	6 March 1967	Washington	9 September 1963
Shincliffe	28 July 1941	Usworth	9 September 1963
Sherburn Colliery	28 July 1941		

Ferryhill Station, August 1936.

The Great North of England Railway (GNER) was authorised in 1836 to build a line from Gateshead to York via Darlington in two sections, the northern one being 34 miles and 34 chains from Gateshead to Croft-on-Tees (two and a half miles south of Darlington) and the southern section being 41 miles and 16 chains from Croft to York. The GNER completed this latter section in 1841 but then failed to build the Darlington to Gateshead section. This led to a conglomeration of companies building their own lines in the area and portions of these, when joined together, gave a somewhat roundabout route from Darlington to Gateshead. Nevertheless they formed the main line from the south to Newcastle from 1844 until the Team Valley line from Gateshead to Tursdale Junction was opened throughout on 15 January 1872.

The old main line was built in four sections: Darlington to Rainton Meadows, opened by the Newcastle & Darlington Junction Railway; Rainton Meadows to Washington, opened by the Durham Junction Railway; Washington to Brockley Whins, opened by the Stanhope & Tyne Railway; and Brockley Whins to Gateshead, opened by the Brandling Junction Railway.

Fencehouses Station.

The line was opened throughout to the public on 19 June 1844 and included a two and a quarter mile branch from Belmont Junction to a station at Durham Gilesgate but both these stations were closed to passenger traffic on 1 April 1857 when a new Durham station was opened on the branch from Leamside to Bishop Auckland. Gilesgate survived as a goods station until around October 1966.

The line's major disadvantage was that it necessitated a reversal at Brockley Whins, from where the line to Gateshead was always very busy. To obviate this a cut-off from Washington to Pelaw was opened on 1 September 1849; this also shortened the distance slightly. The principal engineering feature was a magnificent stone viaduct over the River Wear between Penshaw and Washington. This was known as the Victoria Bridge because the last stone was laid on the day of Queen Victoria's coronation on 28 June 1838. It had four main arches, those at each end being of 100 foot span and the centre two being 144 feet and 160 feet. The total length was 811 feet and the height above high water mark was 135 feet.

With the opening of the Team Valley line in 1868 and its extension to Ferryhill in 1872, which together became the present-day East Coast Main Line, the old main line gradually declined and its stations were closed in the 1960s. The largest, Leamside, had a large island platform with a single bay let in at each end and south of the station was Auckland Junction (latterly Leamside) where the Bishop Auckland branch diverged. Soon after closure the station was demolished and the tracks were straightened.

The Leamside line was mothballed in 1991 after closure of the freightliner terminal at Follingsby; parts of the line were singled and the track was severed at a number of level crossings. However, there are currently proposals by the Tyne & Wear Passenger Transport Authority to reopen the line and some of its stations to ease congestion both on local roads and on the East Coast Main Line itself but so far nothing has happened.

Ferryhill — Port Clarence

Passenger service withdrawn	31 March 1952
Distance	15 ½ miles
Company	Clarence Railway

Stations closed	*Date of closure*
Ferryhill (East Coast Main Line)	6 March 1967
Sedgefield	31 March 1952
Stillington*	31 March 1952

Stations closed	*Date of closure*
Redmarshall **	31 March 1952
Haverton Hill	6 November 1961
Port Clarence	11 September 1939

* Originally named Carlton Ironworks until 1 November 1879.
** Originally named Carlton until 1 July 1923.

Sedgefield Station, 1908.

Redmarshall Station, 1 July 1923.

The Clarence Railway's main line ran from Port Clarence, on the north bank of the Tees opposite Middlesborough, to Stillington North Junction where it divided into branches to Simpasture and Ferryhill whilst, at its eastern end, a branch ran off southwards at Norton to serve Stockton-on-Tees.

Port Clarence signal box, November 1963.

The Clarence's branch thus connected Ferryhill with the Shildon to Newport line and soon carried a significant amount of mineral traffic; this led to the line being widened to four tracks in 1883 from Redmarshall West Junction to Stillington North Junction and led to Carlton and Stillington being rebuilt the following year with island platforms between the up and down passenger lines. At both stations these island platforms served only the northern pair of tracks, leaving the southern pair free for the Shildon to Newport mineral traffic.

Ferryhill — Hartlepool

Passenger service withdrawn	9 June 1952		
Distance	16 ¾ miles		
Company	Great North of England		
	Clarence & Hartlepool Junction Railway		

Stations closed	*Date of closure*	*Stations closed*	*Date of closure*
Ferryhill (East Coast Main Line)	6 March 1967	Wingate	9 June 1952
West Cornforth	9 June 1952	Castle Eden	9 June 1952
Coxhoe Bridge *	9 June 1952	Hesleden	9 June 1952
Trimdon	9 June 1952	Hart **	31 August 1953
		Hartlepool	23 March 1964

* Originally named Coxhoe; re-naming date unknown.
** Closed between 28 July 1941 and 6 May 1946.

Trimdon Station.

The Great North of England, Clarence & Hartlepool Junction Railway (GNECHJR) was formed to join both the Great North of England Railway line and the Clarence Railway's Byers Green branch to the Hartlepool Dock & Railway Company's line near Wingate. However, difficulties arose at the western end of the line where the railway had to cross over the Clarence Railway's Coxhoe branch to reach the latter's Byers Green branch because the Act of Parliament empowering the building of the line did not specifically authorise this crossing. The Clarence Railway promptly seized on this omission as a way to prevent the GNECHJR from completing its line and thus providing a shorter route to the coast. The situation led to physical and legal battles but eventually the GNECHJR succeeded and its line was completed in 1846.

At first there was only an east-to-north connection to the Great North of England main line so that trains from Hartlepool to Ferryhill had to reverse at Thinford Junction but with the completion of a new east-to-south curve in 1873 (in connection with the Spennymoor branch flying junction) trains could at last run direct to Ferryhill. By 1925 there was a service of six trains in each direction between West Hartlepool and Ferryhill, stopping at all stations plus a mail and newspaper train from Ferryhill at 5.43 a.m. The service was doubled on Saturdays and there were two trains in each direction on summer Sundays.

Castle Eden Station.

Leaving Ferryhill the trains ran parallel to the east side of the present-day East Coast Main Line, climbing to the upper junction at Coxhoe Junction and then swinging away to the east to West Cornforth. Beyond Coxhoe Bridge station the line climbed Kelloe Bank which, with a gradient of 1 in 37 in parts, was originally worked by a winding engine; in later years passenger trains climbed the bank unaided but eastbound mineral trains were assisted by the Class J53 0-6-0T engines specifically stationed at Ferryhill for that duty. The level crossing at Trimdon Grange was the site of the original Trimdon station which was resited to the east in 1877/78. East of Wingate the line's ownership changed to the Hartlepool Dock & Railway Company and beyond Castle Eden the line ran down Hesleden Bank on gradients of 1 in 62 and 1 in 52. This incline had originally been rope-worked but this was later replaced by a locomotive line on easier gradients which was built with one track on either side of the old incline.

The passenger service from Ferryhill originally terminated at Hartlepool but with the decline of Hartlepool and the rise of West Hartlepool the trains were diverted to the latter station with a connecting service to Hartlepool. In the 1930s the shuttle service between the two Hartlepool stations was usually worked by Sentinel railcars.

The 1902 timetable shows that there were seven weekday trains between Hartlepool and Ferryhill, plus one on Saturdays that terminated at West Cornforth and another one on Saturday nights from Hartlepool to Trimdon. The Sunday service was two through trains from Hartlepool to Ferryhill and three from Ferryhill.

Stockton — Sunderland via Haswell

Passenger service withdrawn	Stockton to Wellfield: 2 November 1931	*Stations closed*	*Date of closure*
	Wellfield to Sunderland: 5 January 1953	Wellfield	9 June 1952
Distance	26 ½ miles	Thornley	9 June 1952
Company	North Eastern Railway	Shotton Bridge	9 June 1952
		Haswell	9 June 1952
Stations closed	*Date of closure*	South Hetton	9 June 1952
Thorpe Thewles	2 November 1931	Murton Junction	5 January 1953 (see Murton to Durham Elvet)
Wynyard	2 November 1931	Seaton	1 September 1952 (see Murton to Durham Elvet)
Hurworth Burn	2 November 1931	Ryhope	5 January 1953 (see Murton to Durham Elvet)

Shotton Bridge Station.

Shotton Bridge and Station.

STATION, HASWELL.

This line was opened for passenger services from Bowesfield Junction at Stockton through to Wellfield, which served the nearby mining village of Wingate, on 1 March 1880. Here the passenger trains connected with West Hartlepool to Sunderland trains but in 1925 there were only four trains each way per day. The three intermediate stations were very badly sited because both Wynyard and Hurworth Burn were merely areas and served no villages of that name. By contrast, in 1894 the North Eastern Railway gave permission for both Lord and Lady Londonderry, who lived at Wynyard Park, to stop the 7.30 from Newcastle and the 10.30 from York at Thorpe Thewles upon giving notice to the railway authorities. In the early years of the twentieth century this route was used by three trains in each direction on the Newcastle – Liverpool service and by the Newcastle – Oxford service, all of which ran direct from Sunderland to Stockton and thereby missed West Hartlepool.

North of Wellfield the line, which was originally freight only, had been built by the Hartlepool Dock & Railway Company. It passed through Hart and then climbed Hesleden Bank to Haswell where it made an end-on junction with the Durham & Sunderland Railway. It joined the latter's main line at Murton and continued on to its Town Moor station at Sunderland. On the southbound journey trains had to climb Seaton Bank between Sunderland and Ryhope with gradients of 1 in 44 and 1 in 60 for two and a half miles. Southbound trains were banked and northbound ones had to make a momentary stop at Ryhope to ensure that the driver had control before descending the bank. This stop was imposed after a driver lost control on 19 August 1889 and his train was derailed on the curve at the foot of the bank; the enforced stop lasted until 1960. Further south beyond Murton the railway climbed through South Hetton to Haswell. On 1 April 1905 the direct line along the coast between West Hartlepool and Sunderland via Seaham was opened and trains could now run between the two without having to toil up Hesleden Bank in one direction and Seaton Bank in the other.

Murton — Durham Elvet

Passenger service withdrawn   1 January 1931
Distance   8 miles
Company   Durham & Sunderland Railway

Stations closed	*Date of closure*
Hetton	5 January 1953
Pittington	5 January 1953
Sherburn House *	1 January 1931
Durham Elvet	1 January 1931

* Originally named Sherburn until 1 April 1874.

Hetton Station.

A line reached Durham from the east when the Durham & Sunderland Railway opened their line from Sunderland Town Moor to Pittington in 1836. The line reached Sherburn House in 1837 and its terminus at Shincliffe, south of Durham city, on 28 June 1839.

In 1846 the Durham & Sunderland Railway was purchased by the Newcastle & Darlington Junction Railway, who obtained an Act of Parliament for a line running from north of Sherburn to Shincliffe and on to Bishop Auckland. There was to be a triangular junction for access to a station at Elvet in Durham city but the line was never built. Eventually in 1893 the North Eastern Railway did open a station here, which was served by a new line branching off the old Shincliffe line at Sherburn House. From 24 July 1893 the service to Shincliffe was withdrawn and the station closed and at the same time Sherburn House Station was resited from the junction onto the new branch.

Elvet had four platforms and extensive station buildings. In 1925 there were nine trains into and out of the station on weekdays, some running through to Sunderland and others running only to Murton where they made connections with trains to West Hartlepool and Sunderland. However, the passenger service from Pittington to Elvet was not a great success and had a short life of less than forty years as it was withdrawn on 1 January 1931, but Elvet Station continued to be used for one single day every year (except during the war years) until 18 July 1953. That single day was when the famous Durham Miners' Gala was held and special trains were run from most of the surrounding pit villages bringing miners, their families, bands and banners to the city. One of the last uses of the station was by a circus that came by train in 1953.

The line to Pittington remained open until 5 January 1953 and after the closure of Durham Elvet (demolished in 1964) it became the terminus of the service from Sunderland, worked in the 1930s by Class G5 0-4-4T engines and Sentinel railcars. These Class G5s from Sunderland shed were usually the largest locomotives to be seen on the branch but Classes J39 0-6-0s and K1 2-6-0s were used on Miners' Gala specials.

Dunston Branch

Passenger service withdrawn   4 May 1926
Distance   2 ¼ miles
Company   North Eastern Railway

Stations closed	Date of closure
Dunston-on-Tyne *	4 May 1926

* Originally named Dunston until 1 November 1905. Reopened and renamed Dunston on 1 October 1984.

Dunston-on-Tyne Station.

This short branch ran from the south end of the King Edward Bridge in Gateshead and descended, mainly on a gradient of 1 in 100, to join the Low Fell to Dunston line at Norwood Junction. Passenger services commenced on 1 January 1909 and were worked by steam autocars, the journey taking eight minutes. The terminus at Dunston consisted of an island platform with pedestrian access down a ramp from an overbridge carrying the Blaydon – Swalwell – Gateshead road.

The train service was suspended from May 1918 to October 1919 as a wartime measure but it never could compete successfully with the frequent tram service and by 1925 there were only five trains in each direction daily, plus a mid evening and a late evening train on Wednesdays and Saturdays. The service was again suspended 'temporarily' on 4 May 1926 as a result of the General Strike and was never reinstated. However, since the closure of the North Tyneside lines through Scotswood and on the North Wylam Loop, all trains on the Newcastle & Carlisle line now use this route into and out of Newcastle.

Closed passenger stations on lines still open to passengers
Darlington — Newcastle-upon-Tyne (East Coast Main Line)

Stations closed	Date of closure	Stations closed	Date of closure
Aycliffe	2 March 1953	Birtley	5 December 1955
Bradbury	2 January 1950	Lamesley	4 June 1945
Ferryhill	6 March 1967	Low Fell	7 April 1952
Croxdale	26 September 1938	Bensham	5 April 1954
Plawsworth	7 April 1952	Gateshead West	1 November 1965

Aycliffe Station.

Stockton-on-Tees — Newcastle-upon-Tyne via Sunderland *

Stations closed	Date of closure	Stations closed	Date of closure
Norton-on-Tees	7 March 1960	Ryhope East ***	7 March 1960
Greatham	24 November 1991	Monkwearmouth	6 March 1967
Hart **	31 August 1953		
Blackhall Rocks	4 January 1960		
Blackhall Colliery	4 May 1964		
Horden	4 May 1964		
Easington	4 May 1964		

* Stations north of Monkwearmouth have been converted or rebuilt into stations on the Tyne & Wear Metro.

** Closed between 28 July 1941 and 6 May 1946.

*** Originally named Ryhope until April 1959.

Greatham Station.

SILKSWORTH

65894

A coal train with snowplough passing the old 'Londonderry' station, a private halt for Seaham Hall, north of Seaham, March 1967.

Stockton-on-Tees — Newcastle-upon-Tyne via Sunderland